Art All Around Us

CLOTHING DESIGN AND FASHION

Ezra E. Knopp

CREATED BY Humans

Published in 2026 by The Rosen Publishing Group, Inc.
2544 Clinton Street, Buffalo, NY 14224

First Edition

Editor: Greg Roza
Designer: Rachel Rising

Photo Credits: Cover, Prostock-studio/Shutterstock.com; Cover, (series background) Yuliya Chsherbakova/Shutterstock.com; p. 5 Media_Photos/Shutterstock.com; p. 7 Duerte Robert/Shutterstock.com; p. 7 Charlotte ten Haave/Shutterstock.com; p. 7 DELBO ANDREA/Shuttertock.com; p. 9 Jade ThaiCatwalk/Shutterstock.com; p. 9 liza1979/Shutterstock.com; p. 10 https://commons.wikimedia.org/wiki/File:Zentralbibliothek_Z%C3%BCrich_-_Merckliche_Beschreibung_sampt_eygenlicher_Abbildung_eynes_frembden_unbekanten_Volcks_-_000003625_(cropped).jpg; p. 11 Fab4Shutterstock/Shutterstock.com; p. 13 https://commons.wikimedia.org/wiki/File:Eustache_Le_Sueur_-_Caligula_Depositing_the_Ashes_of_his_Mother_and_Brother_in_the_Tomb_of_his_Ancestors_-_WGA12607.jpg; p. 14 https://commons.wikimedia.org/wiki/File:Portrait_of_Charles_Frederick_Worth_aged_30.jpg; p. 15 https://commons.wikimedia.org/wiki/File:Marie-Antoinette;_koningin_der_Fransen.jpg; pp. 17, 19 Sam Aronov/Shutterstock.com; p. 18 https://commons.wikimedia.org/wiki/File:Alice_Joyce_wearing_antique_gold_emb._in_rubies_LCCN2014719071.jpg; p. 18 https://commons.wikimedia.org/wiki/File:Empress_Eug%C3%A9nie_in_Court_Dress_(Guillemet_after_Winterhalter,_Mus%C3%A9e_d%27Orsay).jpg; p. 19 FashionStock.com/Shutterstock.com; p. 19 neftali/Shutterstock.com; p. 20 New Africa/Shutterstock.com; pp. 21, 22 Chaosamran_Studio/Shutterstock.com; p. 23 AntonStyle/Shuttertock.com; p. 23 Gorodenkoff/Shutterstock.com; p. 24 ANTONIO TRUZZI/Shutterstock.com; p. 25 Krakenimages.com/Shutterstock.com; p. 26 Dejan Dundjerski/Shutterstock.com; p. 27 PeopleImages.com - Yuri A/Shutterstock.com; p. 29 BearFotos/Shutterstock.com.

Cataloging-in-Publication Data
Names: Knopp, Ezra E.
Title: Clothing design and fashion / Ezra E. Knopp.
Description: Buffalo, NY : Created by Humans, an imprint of Rosen Publishing, 2026. | Series: Art all around us | Includes glossary and index.
Identifiers: ISBN 9781534552722 (pbk.) | ISBN 9781534552739 (library bound) | ISBN 9781534552746 (ebook)
Subjects: LCSH: Fashion design--Juvenile literature. | Fashion--Juvenile literature. | Clothing and dress--Juvenile literature.
Classification: LCC TT507.K655 2026 | DDC 746.92--dc23

Manufactured in the United States of America

CPSIA Compliance Information: Batch #CWCBH26. For Further Information contact Rosen Publishing at 1-800-237-9932.

CONTENTS

TRULY FABULOUS ART! 4
DESIGN, DESIGNERS, AND THE INDUSTRY 6
KINDS OF FASHION DESIGN 8
A BRIEF HISTORY OF CLOTHING 10
THE MODERN FASHION INDUSTRY 16
FASHION THROUGH THE YEARS 18
DESIGN SKILLS 20
FASHION SKETCHING 22
SEWING SKILLS 24
IS IT ART? 26
THE FASHION DESIGNER IN YOU 28
GLOSSARY 30
FOR MORE INFORMATION 31
INDEX 32

TRULY FABULOUS ART!

We live in a colorful world filled with works of art created by all kinds of people. Museums display paintings and sculptures from throughout history. Radio, television, and online resources play music, show music videos, and feature-length films. Even the clothes we wear every day are a form of **artistic expression**. The height of artistic expression using clothing is often referred to as haute couture (French for "high sewing").

Fashion and clothing design reflect trends in our society, and sometimes honor past fashion styles with new designs using old looks or ways. Let's learn about the range of human creativity though the clothes we create and wear.

Some people enjoy displaying their individuality through the clothes they wear. Some people like making their own clothes!

DESIGN, DESIGNERS, AND THE INDUSTRY

You might be thinking: *Aren't fashion and fashion design the same thing?* It's true that they can seem like one and the same, but fashion, as an **industry**, is much more than the designs themselves. It's also the artists, styles, materials, and models that make fashion the respected artform it has become.

Designers are the superstars of the fashion industry. People like Coco Chanel, Giorgio Armani, and Carolina Herrera have the artistic talent and skill to create forward-thinking designs people will love. These artists have each left a lasting mark on fashion and will be celebrated, and copied, for years to come.

Giorgio Armani

GIORGIO ARMANI

Italian designer Giorgio Armani founded the fashion house Armani in Milan, Italy, in 1975. His designs are still wildly popular.

KINDS OF FASHION DESIGN

Haute couture refers to hand-crafted, custom clothing made from expensive fabrics. There are specific rules for this kind of fashion. For example, fashion houses, or labels, must have a studio in Paris, France, that has at least 15 employees. They must also present at least 35 creations twice a year at fashions shows.

Prêt-à-porter (French for "ready-to-wear") design is similar to haute couture in that it uses quality materials and close attention to detail. Ready-to-wear designs are also displayed at fashion shows. However ready-to-wear designs are produced in standard sizes. They aren't custom designs.

The third kind of fashion design is called mass market. These are the standard-sized clothes most people buy in stores and online. Mass-market clothing can be artistic and affordable!

A BRIEF HISTORY OF CLOTHING

Clothing was first a matter of survival, not fashion. Our knowledge of prehistory clothing is spotty. Fabrics usually don't last for thousands of years like pottery and arrowheads do. However, **archaeologists** have found **artifacts** related to clothes, such as sewing needles made of bone. Scientists have also discovered fossilized shoeprints that are tens of thousands of years old.

The first clothes were loose objects such as capes and loincloths. They provided some protection from the weather, but not much. People began making clothing with sleeves and pantlegs. Other clothing items followed, including hats and shoes.

The Inuit and the Yupik people live in or close to the Arctic Circle. Long ago they created special snow goggles. They cut narrow slits into strips of driftwood or bone to block the sun's glare.

For centuries, most clothes were plain but useful. In time, clothes became a symbol of power or wealth. This can be seen in the clothing from ancient Egypt, Greece, and Rome. Political and religious leaders often wore clothing made from rare fabrics and dyes. However, the clothing of average people was far less costly and colorful. It remained protective and **utilitarian**.

The fashion industry itself arose in the 1600s. New tailoring techniques led to new, more exciting fashions. Haute couture and prêt-à-porter clothing became more popular and **unique**. Some fabrics became more popular in Europe in the 1600s. These included silk and velvet.

Purple fabric was once considered a sign of wealth and power. This is because purple dye was rare and expensive for many years.

The **Industrial Revolution** began in Europe around 1730. Many technical and mechanical advances helped shape the growing fashion industry. New tools and quicker manufacturing processes resulted in cheaper clothing for the average person. Important names in fashion from this time include Rose Bertin, Queen Marie Antoinette's personal dressmaker.

Charles Frederick Worth is widely considered the first modern fashion designer. He started the idea of fashion houses where designers could show off their work and where **clients** could have clothes made to order. It wasn't long before fashion shows became a popular way to celebrate fashion creations.

Charles Frederick Worth

Marie Antoinette posed in her elegant dresses for many portraits.

Marie Antoinette—The First Fashionista

Marie Antoinette (French queen from 1774 to 1792) had a great influence on the start of the fashion industry. She spent a lot of money on clothes and jewels at a time when French people were struggling in many ways. Antoinette was often **criticized** for her fashion sense, but her style was also widely copied by wealthy ladies of the time.

THE MODERN FASHION INDUSTRY

Fashion houses quickly grew in popularity. Some of the oldest labels still in business today include the French label Hermès (established 1837), the English label Burberry (1856), and the American label Brooks Brothers (1818). Throughout the 1900s and into the 2000s, designers have revolutionized the fashion industry. Figures such as Christian Dior, Coco Chanel, Mary Quant, and Yves Saint Laurent helped keep the tidal wave of fashion **innovation** surging ahead.

Fashion magazines helped bring more fashion to the masses, and glamorous fashion shows continue to amaze people. Today, modern technology, especially computers, have given younger designers far more tools to work with.

Many designers craft wildly imaginative clothing made exclusively for fashion shows and museums. Would you wear one of these outfits to school?

FASHION THROUGH THE YEARS

Charles Frederick Worth circa 1855

The Roaring 20s

Mary
Quant
1960s

Anna Sui
1990s
25

Contemporary
Fashion Show
2025

DESIGN SKILLS

Fashion designers have a great admiration for clothing **aesthetics** and unique styles. This comes from years of observing clothing styles and fashion trends. They're good at conceptualizing, or forming a unique plan for a new project. Designers understand body proportions and can adjust designs to different body types to ensure that everyone looks fabulous.

Fashion designers don't need to be skilled drawers. However, most learn to create quick fashion sketches. It just takes some practice and basic knowledge of fashion styles. Today, many designers use computer programs to create sketches and experiment with styles.

You can also find free fashion examples online. You can learn to create your own by using them to practice.

FASHION SKETCHING

Before a designer sketches a new design, they draw a croquis (French for "sketch"). This is a stick figure. The designer starts with simple shapes, such as an oval for the head, a triangle for the torso, and a long rectangle for the waist. Once the croquis is complete, it's time to design!

When creating a fashion sketch, the designer thinks about clothing style, fit, arm length, and more. When you get better, you can start to experiment with poses.

SEWING SKILLS

Once the design is finalized, it's time to start creating fashion! Although not all designers sew their own creations, most have a solid understanding of sewing skills. Some fashion designers are masters at sewing! They use a wide range of tools, from the noble needle and thread to the newest electric sewing machines.

Designers understand all kinds of fabrics—how they feel, how expensive they are, how easy they are to use, and even how they're made. They often have to make last-minute measurements and changes to their creations based on the model they use.

Designers need to meet deadlines, which could be a big show or client's wedding. They are good working in stressful situations.

How to Hone Your Skills

There are several ways you can develop your sewing skills. There are fashion schools and organizations that can help you prepare for a career in clothing design. But there are other ways. The best way is to get your hands on fabric, needles, and thread and start practicing. Check for local "sewing clubs" in your area where you can meet others with your interests. Many online sources offer advice and guidance as well.

IS IT ART?

Not every designer becomes a huge success with their own fashion house. And that's OK! The world needs fashion designers who make mass-marketed clothing. We need designers to make wedding dresses and prom gowns, business suits and tuxedos. Some designers even go into costume design. They are often hired by people who create movies, plays, and musicals.

There are those who insist "high art" fashion only occurs on the runways of Paris and Milan. They may argue that a local wedding dress "seamstress" doesn't create art. This is an ongoing debate in the world of fashion! What do you think?

Many people believe fashion is both useful as well as artistic. Designers help us all show off who we are!

THE FASHION DESIGNER IN YOU

Do you like the colorful world of fashion design? Do you have basic sewing and drawing skills? Do you enjoy mixing and matching clothing to create the perfect "you" look? Then you definitely have what it takes to be a fashion designer!

You are now prepared to think like a designer. What's your dream project? Designers are very good at conceptualizing clothing in their mind, but there's more! What kinds of fabrics would you use? What colors do you prefer? Will your creation need buttons? What types of clothing design will you take **inspiration** from? The sky's the limit when showing off your talent for fashion!

Practicing with a sewing machine is a great way to hone your sewing skills. Many libraries have sewing machines you can use or borrow!

GLOSSARY

aesthetic: A pleasing appearance or effect.
archaeologist: One who studies past human life based on what those people left behind.
artifact: A usually simple object (such as a tool) showing human work and representing a culture or a stage in the development of a culture.
artistic expression: The act and process of showing what you think and how you feel though art.
client: A person who uses the professional advice or services of another.
criticize: To examine and judge something.
Industrial Revolution: An era of social and economic changes marked by advances in technology and science.
industry: A group of businesses that provide a certain product or service.
innovation: A new invention, or a new way of doing things.
inspiration: Something that moves someone to do great things.
unique: One of a kind.
utilitarian: Having to do with something that is useful rather than beautiful.

FOR MORE INFORMATION

BOOKS

Quigley, Kerri. *Fashion Design for Kids: Skill-Building Activities for Future Fashion Designers*. New York, NY: Calisto Books, 2021.

Wilson, Lakita. *My Fierce Fashion*. Minneapolis, MN: Learner Publications, 2022.

WEBSITES

Fashion
kids.britannica.com/students/article/fashion/274273
Read a less-brief history of fashion here.

What Is a Croquis?
www.masterclass.com/articles/what-is-a-croquis-learn-how-to-draw-croquis-with-detailed-step-by-step-guide
Learn more about drawing a croquis at this detailed website.

Publisher's note to educators and parents: Our editors have carefully reviewed these websites to ensure that they are suitable for students. Many websites change frequently, however, and we cannot guarantee that a site's future contents will continue to meet our high standards of quality and educational value. Be advised that students should be closely supervised whenever they access the internet.

INDEX

A
Armani, Giorgio, 6, 7

B
Bertin, Rose, 14

C
Chanel, Coco, 6, 16
clients, 14, 25

D
Dior, Christian, 16

F
fabric, 8, 10, 12, 13, 14, 25, 28
fashion house, 8, 14, 16, 26
fashion show, 8, 14, 16, 17, 25
fashion sketch, 20, 22, 23

H
haute couture, 4, 8, 12
Herrera, Carolina, 6
history, 10, 11, 12, 13

M
mass market, 9, 26

P
prêt-à-porter, 8, 12

Q
Quant, Mary, 16, 19

S
Saint Laurent, Yves, 16
sewing machine, 24, 29
sewing needle, 10, 24, 25
Sui, Anna, 19

W
Worth, Charles Frederick, 14, 18